William Torrey Harris

How to teach natural Science in public Schools

William Torrey Harris

How to teach natural Science in public Schools

ISBN/EAN: 9783337024932

Printed in Europe, USA, Canada, Australia, Japan

Cover: Foto ©Paul-Georg Meister /pixelio.de

More available books at **www.hansebooks.com**

HOW TO TEACH

NATURAL SCIENCE

IN

PUBLIC SCHOOLS

WM. T. HARRIS, LL. D.

COMMISSIONER OF EDUCATION

Second Edition, from New Plates

SYRACUSE, N. Y.

C. W. BARDEEN, PUBLISHER

1895

NOTE BY THE PUBLISHER

This plan of study was first issued by Dr. Harris in 1871. It appeared in his Report for that year (pp. 173–181, and xlviii-lvii), and also as a Syllabus of Lessons for the teachers, document No. 34. It appeared next in the annual Report for 1877 of Superintendent Philbrick, of Boston (pp. 94–102), where he speaks of this syllabus as the characteristic of the St. Louis course, "so interesting and important that I quote it in full." It was again reprinted in the St. Louis report for 1879, and finally has been made the basis of the report of the Committee on Physics-Teaching, presented at the meeting of the National Educational Association, Chicago, 1887.

It is by request of Charles K. Wead, chairman of this Committee, that the syllabus is now reprinted in form accessible to all; and since it has been accepted for sixteen years as the best presentation of the subject, it unquestionably belongs among "School-Room Classics".

It is published by consent of Dr. Harris, and in form according with his suggestions.

SYRACUSE, *June, 1887.*

NOTE TO THE SECOND EDITION

New plates being required, a larger and more open page has been given to this little manual, which has proved of such service all over the country.

SYRACUSE, *Nov. 10, 1894.*

CONTENTS

REPORT TO THE BOARD OF EDUCATION............... 9

Natural science as an instrument of modern civilization.............................. 10

The compass of natural science....................11

The order of instruction.....................……..12

Method of teaching...............................13

SPECIAL REPORT TO THE BOARD....................…........16

    I. Not everything can be taught..............16

    II. The school must furnish theoretical insight...17

    III. Reading, arithmetic, geography...........18

    IV. Grammar, history............................18

    V. Sciences, mathematics, other languages..19

    VI. Higher studies in the elementary course..20

    VII. Social and natural sciences..................20

    VIII. Elements of the natural sciences in elementary schools.............................21

    IX. Outlines and reference books..............22

    X. A course of study...................23, 28–35

    XI. Oral vs. text-book method.................23

    XII. Advantages of the oral method...........24

XIII. Advantages of the text-book method.....24

XIV. Points to be observed in recitation........24

XV. The teacher should not use the text-book
in recitation....................... 26

COURSE OF INSTRUCTION...............................28

First year, plants.....................................28

Second year, animals................................28

Third year, elements of physical nature........29

Fourth year, botany.................................30

Fifth year, zoölogy, physiology and hygiene....31

Sixth year, physical geography...................33

Seventh year, physics..............................34

ON THE METHOD OF TEACHING.......................36

Method rather than quantity......................37

The number of topics............. 37

General plan of the course........................38

1. The subjects......................,...............38

2. Recurrence of topics...........................38

3. Appearance of the sciences in outline......39

4. Illustrative objects must be typical........39

5. The perceptive powers developed...........39

6. How to conduct a lesson.......................40

7. How to use reference books.................41

8. Incidental teaching...........................43

9. The study of Man to be parallel...........44

How to Teach Natural Science in Public Schools

In former reports I have discussed at length the
significance of the common branches of study and
have endeavored to show that even the rudiments,
such as reading, writing, arithmetic and geography,
are of inestimable importance. Their acquirement
works a more potent change in the individual than
any subsequent step in his culture. That these
rudiments can almost be said to add faculties to
the child's mind ; that they are so general—so wide
reaching in their application—as to lie at the basis
of further progress in education ; that their claims
surpass in every respect those of other special
branches that have been urged for admission to the
district school course of study on the ground that
they are " more practical " : these and other posi-
tions have been stated and supported by argument.
It remains in this report to present the scheme by
which the claims of these special branches have
been recognized in our course of study without

compromising the thoroughness of the regular instruction in the conventional rudiments above named.

It was clearly seen that the problem demanded an introduction of a popular course of instruction in natural science in such a way as to react beneficially not only upon the pupil's progress in the regular course, but also upon the teacher's methods and practical skill in imparting information.

NATURAL SCIENCE AS AN INSTRUMENT OF MODERN CIVILIZATION

Granting the importance of natural science as furnishing the theoretical basis of productive industry and the consequent elevation of the masses of all the people by means of wealth created thereby, the first question in making a course of study was to bring before the mind the entire field in classified form. The obvious division into Physics and Natural History—the former including the department that deals with elements in their mathematical relations, and the latter including the descriptive treatment of the world as it exists in multiplicity and variety of special existences— suggests at once two compendious treatisies long in use in our higher schools: Natural Philosophy, furnishing the outline of Physics; and Physical Geography, furnishing a similar outline of Natural History. Again, Physics in its broadest acceptation divides into a science of the movement of masses and that of molecular motion. Chemistry thus forms a kind of transition to Natural History. Natural History, again, treats the world as organic: first the process of the elements, including the geological and meteorological processes (taken in their widest compass); second the plant, and third the animal.

THE COMPASS OF NATURAL SCIENCE

Having thus mapped out the domain of natural science so that our course of study shall not arbitrarily adopt one or more provinces to the neglect of others equally important, the next problem was to ascertain what phases of these several departments are suitable for popular exposition and are easily illustrated. Ascertaining this, it became necessary to sketch out the course in such a way as to make several complete circuits during the seven years of the district school course. The lowest one should seize certain striking features in each

department—making a strong impression and silent-
ly determining the mind to reflection and observation in the domain of Natural Science.   The second
course must travel round in the same path, but
more systematically and in detail.   The third one,
still deepening and generalizing the ideas of the
pupil, would make the effects permanent.   Three
courses were fixed upon for this reason.   The seven
years of the district school course thus allowed three
years each to be given to the first and second course,
and two years for the third.   Inasmuch as the
subjects were taken up with a considerable degree
of scientific strictness in the High School, the courses
of study in natural sciences would now extend from
the commencement in the primary schools to the
last year of the High School.   A pupil, coming
into any grade in the schools and remaining three
years, would know something of each of the great
departments of Nature.

THE ORDER OF INSTRUCTION IN NATURAL SCIENCE

The first year, lowest grade, in the schools began
with lessons on the plant; the second year was
taken up with animals, and especially the structure
of the human body; while the third year initiated

the pupils into physical forces in various familiar applications, and made some progress in considering the geological and meteorological elements, such as earth, air, fire, and water. In the fourth, fifth, and sixth years the course took a more practical turn. While in the first three years it had dealt chiefly with the rationale of the child's playthings and such phenomena as excited his astonishment, in the second course he was to learn to understand what is useful to man in these departments. In the sixth and seventh years the maturity of the pupil allows him to investigate with some degree of scientific interest, and hence the more general form is adopted.

METHOD OF TEACHING NATURAL SCIENCE

The important question to be settled was how to bring in these lessons so as not to distract and dissipate the attention of teacher and pupil from other work. Fatal dissipation of energies follows from undertaking too many subjects at a time. If the teacher has to pass daily from arithmetic to a lesson on natural science, it is likely that one or both these lessons will suffer. Accordingly, instead of introducing these lessons daily, they were confined to one afternoon of each week, and sufficient time given to each lesson to allow a deep and lasting impression to be made. Whereas, in ordinary lessons the pupil is required to be so intensely active that he cannot sustain the exertion for more than thirty minutes, in the natural science lesson he is to give his attention for one hour ; but the teacher is so to vary the lesson by lecture, experiment, reading interesting descriptions, conversation with the pupils on their experience, that the class shall be able to do this without excessive fatigue. By this arrangement each lesson becomes for the teacher a practical experiment in the art of instruction ; and when the pupils are allowed to become listless, the teacher sees her inefficiency portrayed before her and must make greater effort next time.

It seems to me that this phase of the subject—its value to the teacher—is worth quite as much as the immediate value of these lessons to the pupil. I do not lose sight of the fact that he gains from week to week an impression that deepens into practical scientific thought in after years. But the teacher is led to study and thoroughly prepare herself, and then in that lesson she is led to probe in a freer manner than ordinary the miscellaneous fund of experience possessed by the individuals of her class; thus she cannot fail to find new means of getting hold of pupils in each of the regular branches of the daily course. She will find herself getting more and more emancipated from the slavish use of the text-book, and able to stand before her class with a consciousness of her strength and ability to draw out the resources of each and all of her pupils and combine the same into one result.

Thus an attempt has been made to introduce the study of the sciences with all their infinitude of detail, so as to act as a stimulant on the regular course, as regards both teacher and pupil. It is thought that the pupil will receive even more benefit indirectly through the increased efficiency of the daily instruction than from the weekly lessons, and yet that these lessons themselves will be far more effective than if given in short object- . lessons of fifteen minutes per day.

The details of instruction and of the course, together with a synoptic view of it, are given in the appendix of the report.* I insert here my special report to the Board on the subject, in order to present the other phases of the subject,

* In this edition on pp. 28 to 46.

not already commented on in the remarks just made.

SPECIAL REPORT TO THE BOARD

GENTLEMEN,—Inasmuch as the first half-quarter of the present scholastic year has sufficed to get our schools into fair running order, and to lay out the plan of a new system of school organization which promises to furnish a frame-work on which the schools under your charge may grow to an indefinite extent, the occasion seems to be auspicious for the consideration of certain matters relating to the course of study and the methods of instruction to be followed by the pupils and teachers.

That these are great and weighty matters in education every educator knows well, and none better than the members of your honorable body, as is manifest by the interest shown here from time to time in securing the best text-books and the introduction of the most important branches of study into our course.

I therefore beg leave to offer the following remarks and suggestions for your approval, and for adoption in case of approval :

I.   And first it will be conceded, I think, that we cannot teach everything in the short period devoted for schooling. Even were the period of schooling much longer than it really is, there are many things learned much better out of school than in it—many things learned much better at home, or in the field or workshop than in a school-room. But with our short school period, lasting on the average for five years with us in the city, and about three years, more or less, in the country, there is the utmost need of the most careful selection of what is essential. The course of study must contain only what the pupil is not likely to pick up from intercourse with the family circle, with his fellow playmates, or with his fellow workmen. More than this, it must contain only such matters as have a general theoretic bearing on the world in which he lives, and the institutions and character of the human species of which the pupil is an individual.

II. It is clear then, that the school must furnish the pupil theoretical insight. Here is a common ground, and it is practical to give the pupil a knowledge of general elements which he may apply in after life to any one of the many trades or professions. Every boy and girl will find a knowledge of reading, writing, arithmetic, and geography useful in any sphere of life that either he or she may be called to fill. Whatever occupation they may follow, these branches will assist them. And what is said of these elementary branches is likewise true of the habits of character formed in a well-disciplined school, such as order, neatness, cleanliness, earnestness, industry, punctuality, self-respect, self-control, obedience to rule, kindness, forbearance, courtesy, considerateness, affability and politeness, sympathy and love.

III. I do not think there is much ground for dispute as to the order for these elementary studies. Reading comes first, for by it the pupil becomes able to pursue independent study, and thus to add to what he receives orally from his teacher. Arithmetic may begin almost as early as reading, and writing should not be delayed at all. Geography should begin as soon as the pupil learns to read with some facility. Compared with other branches, these simplest elements are by far the most important, and nothing should interfere with their most speedy acquisition. They are in themselves the tools which assist in acquiring all other knowledge.

IV. Of man's instruments the most wonderful is language. His whole rational existence depends upon it. Some special study of the structure of

this wonderful instrumentality has been found
essential in all systems of education. Hence, we
place the study of grammar next in importance
after the four elements. History well succeeds grammar, for grammar prepares the way for it by analyz-
ing the structure of the human mind, as exhibited
and mirrored in language. How the human character unfolds in time is shown in history. Knowledge of men is more important than knowledge of
things, as we all find when we grow up and try to
succeed in life. We learn that we can do nothing
nor achieve anything without the aid and consent
of our fellow men. We must, therefore, understand
the springs and motives of human action, both the
permanent ones and the ones that control tem-
porarily.

V. Above and beyond these just-named studies,
which form a complete elementary course, such as
has been wisely laid down by your rules as consti-
tuting the course of study for the district schools
—above and beyond these follows the study of
the sciences, of the higher mathematics, of those
languages from which our own is derived or which
are kindred to it, and the literature thereof. These
studies in their proper development form the higher

course of study, and are commenced in the high school.

VI. Now arises the important question :   Should any or all of these higher studies be introduced into the elementary course?   It is clear that in their proper form they cannot. The study of foreign language by its structure ought to be preceded by some study of the native tongue.   The study of the ' higher mathematics ought to be preceded by that of arithmetic; so literature cannot be well studied without a knowledge of the rudiments of geography, history and grammar, to say nothing of reading and writing.

VII.   The sciences are twofold : the human, *i. e.*, social and political sciences, including political economy, pedagogy and the like, on the one hand, and natural sciences on the other. The human sciences require the highest maturity of thought for their mastery. The natural sciences, which are divided into physics (including the sciences defining inorganic and organic nature, the plant, the animal, and man), imply first, a direct application of mathematics, and secondly, an indirect application of the same in order to comprehend the working of the instruments through which nature is observed and classified. Hence it is evident that so far as complete study and exhaustive survey are concerned, the place for the sciences is in the higher course, as has been determined by the rules of the Board.

VIII. But there is a further question to settle: Can we not give those children who study five years or a less time in our schools, some outlines of Physics and Natural History, which will be of great service to them in after life, and for the time being not interfere seriously with the prosecution of elementary studies?

This question I answer in the affirmative, on the following grounds: The value of all higher studies is two-fold, one as giving us the practical mastery over their spheres through a complete comprehension of them scientifically; the other as giving us a technical mastery over their spheres, thereby adding to our general culture, or as we express it, "general information". For instance, it is not necessary to be thoroughly and scientifically an astronomer to read with pleasure and profit the third volume of Humboldt's Cosmos, or indeed most writings on the subject of astronomy. But without an elementary course of some sort in astronomy, these works would be sealed books. The general ideas of a science and its mode of procedure and its technics may be acquired with little labor; nay it may be a mere pastime to do this. On this ground we may introduce certain outlines of Natural History and Natural Philosophy into lower grades of our schools. But it must be introduced in such a way as to afford relief from the other studies, and not be placed in the same rank with them.

IX. To illustrate my meaning, and with a sincere desire to furnish what seems to be demanded by the community, I have sketched the following outlines, following therein the reference books you have provided for your teachers and with special regard to the resources which they furnish. These reference books are Brande's Encyclopedia, Draper's Physiology, Tate's Natural Philosophy, Wells's Natural Philosophy, Hotz's First Lesson's in Physics, Hooker's Child's Book of Nature, Guyot's Earth and Man, Calkins's Primary Object Lessons, Youman's First Book in Botany, Warren's Physical Geography. It is desirable, in my opinion, that you may add to these a set of colored charts illustrative of the anatomy of plants and animals—one set for each school. That these lessons should be oral, conducted by description and illustration on the part of the teacher, and impressed on the minds of the pupils by question and answer, and free conversation, seems to me the proper mode by all means. And inasmuch as this exercise should serve as a kind of recreation and relaxation from the regular course, I recommend that one hour be set apart for it on each Wednesday afternoon in each room in the district schools.

X. [Here follows the syllabus of lessons in natural science given on pp. 28 to 35.]

In recommending the above course, I would guard especially against any bad effects it might have in diminishing the strictness of the regular course of study by confining it to one hour each week, and by insisting upon the use of the purely oral method by the teacher.

XI. The use of the oral method in this case suggests the question: What is the difference between the oral and the so-called text-book method, and what are the merits and defects of each?

In the former, the oral method, the teacher is the general source of information; in the latter, or text-book method, the pupil is sent to the book for information. In neither of these methods is cramming of memory with mere words considered to be good teaching, and yet it may happen under a poor teacher, whether the oral or text-book method is used.

XII.   The excellence of the oral method should be its freedom from stiffness and pedantry, and its drawing out of the pupil to self-activity in a natural manner.   Its abuse happens when in the hands of a poor teacher the subject is presented in a confused manner, or scientific precision is lost by using too familiar language or by too much pouring-in without enough exercising the pupil by making him do the reciting and explanation.

XIII.   The excellence of the text-book method consists in getting the pupil to work instead of working for him ; in teaching him how to study for himself and to overcome difficulties by himself, instead of solving them for him.   Unless the teacher knows this and directs all his efforts to achieve this end, very great abuses creep in.   Thus it may happen that the teacher requires the pupil merely to memorize the words of the book, and does not insist upon any clear understanding of it. Indolent teachers lean upon the text-book and neglect to perform their own part of the recitation.

XIV.   But in the hands of the good teacher the

text-book is a powerful instrument to secure industry, precision, accuracy, and self-help on the part of the pupil. In conducting a recitation the teacher should :

1st. See that the main point is brought out, explained and illustrated again and again by the different pupils, each in his own language, and the using of the language of the book discouraged in so far as it tends to verbatim or parrot-like recitation.

2d. The teacher should himself criticise, and call upon his pupils to criticise, the defects made in the statements by each pupil, so that they shall acquire a habit of alertness in noticing inaccuracy as well as lack of exhaustiveness in definition, whether in oral statements or in the text-book itself.

3d. The lesson should in all cases be brought home to the pupil's own experience, and his own observation and reflection made to verify the statement of the books.

4th. Every recitation should connect the lessons of to-day to the lessons already recited, and the questions awakened in to-day's lessons should be skilfully managed to arouse interest in the subject of to-morrow's lesson.

5th. The good teacher always notes by the recitation of a pupil what are his habits of study, and the recitation is the place where bad habits are pointed out, and the true method of study shown and illustrated.

XV. I think all will agree with me in pronouncing the recitation conducted in the manner here described effective in securing the ends for which you have established the rules and regulations governing the teachers in the public schools. I have now to point out an additional regulation, which, if adopted by your honorable body, will, I think, lead to the correction of some of the abuses more or less prevalent among the teachers of our schools. I refer to the practice of some of our teachers of using the text-book during the recitation as a source of information from which to draw a supply for their own use on the occasion, thus making up for their own lack of preparation. From this practice results the greater bulk of the evils complained of by intelligent parents, who find their children becoming mere cramming machines, instead of intelligent investigators. That the teacher should know at least as much of the lesson as the pupil, does not need statement. Why, then, should the teacher have recourse to the text while the pupil is debarred

from it?   In consideration of the evils arising from
this source, I respectfully suggest the adoption of a
regulation prohibiting to the teacher the use of the
text-book in the recitation whenever the pupil is
expected to recite without the book; and that the
teacher be recommended to use a syllabus of topics
or questions, either written or printed, in the conduct of such recitations.

COURSE OF INSTRUCTION

FIRST YEAR OR GRADE
PLANTS OR OUTLINE OF BOTANY

First Quarter. Flowers, their structure, color, perfume, habit, and shapes. Inasmuch as the pupils of this grade enter school in the early fall or spring, their first quarter's work can be illustrated directly from the garden.

Second Quarter. Leaves, fruits, seeds ; shape, uses, sap, decay.

Third Quarter. Buds, roots, their purpose ; stalks and trunks, bark of plants, wood.

Fourth Quarter. Circulation of sap, what is made from sap, sleep of plants, etc. Review of topics of the year.

SECOND YEAR OR GRADE
ANIMALS, OR OUTLINES OF ZOÖLOGY AND
PHYSIOLOGY

First Quarter. Blood ; what it makes ; how it is made. The ground ; what comes from it as food for animals; stomach and teeth. Circulation of the blood.

Second Quarter. Breathing; brain and nerves; use of the senses; seeing; protection of the eyes; hearing; smell; taste; touch; the bones; muscles.

Third Quarter. Brains and nerves in animals compared with those in man; limbs of animals, and their uses; the hand in man, and its substitutes in animals; what instruments and tools animals possess for attack and defence.

Fourth Quarter. Wings and fins; clothing of man and animals; wherein man is superior to animals; intelligence 'of animals; sleep, its uses; death, what it is. Review of topics for the year.

THIRD GRADE OR YEAR

ELEMENTS OF PHYSICAL NATURE

First Quarter. Air; wind; flying and swimming compared; pressure of the air; pumps; barometer, air-pumps, pop-guns; gases distinguished from liquids; gun-powder.

Second Quarter. Balloons; bubbles; heated air; chimneys; draft and ventilation; uses of water; water level; pressure of water; attractions in solids and liquids.

Third Quarter. Water in the air, clouds, snow, frost and ice; heat and cold; communication or conduction of heat; effects of heat; steam; light; color; electricity; magnetism.

Fourth Quarter. Gravitation; motion of the earth; friction. Review of the year's work.

FOURTH YEAR OR GRADE

BOTANY MORE SYSTEMATICALLY STUDIED

First Quarter. Modes of studying parts of PLANTS; leaf, stem, inflorescence, flower, root, seed, woody plants, fruit, illustrating by familiar examples.

Second Quarter. The difference in species of TREES; their habits, place of growth and use of man; pine, cedar, willow, oak, beech, maple, walnut, hickory, sycamore, ash, poplar, birch (what "deciduous" and "evergreen" signify), magnolia, live-oak, honey-locust, banyan, laurel, mosses.

Third Quarter. FOOD PLANTS: 1. Wheat, barley, oats, rye, Indian corn, rice. 2. Potatoes, yams, beets, turnips, onions, beans, peas. 3. Apples, peaches, pears, plums, cherries, oranges, bananas, lemons, bread-fruit, dates, pine-apples, figs, grapes. 4. Sago, tapioca, sugar-cane, cocoanut palm (its various uses). 5. Pepper, cinnamon, cloves, nutmeg, vanilla.   6. Tea, coffee, cocoa, maté.   7. Iceland moss.

Fourth Quarter. PLANTS USEFUL IN THE ARTS :
1. Indigo, logwood.   2. Olive (oil), flaxseed (oil), pine, turpentine, rosin, tar.   3. Caoutchouc, gutta percha.   MEDICINAL PLANTS AND STIMULANTS : Sarsaparilla, cinchona (quinine), aloe, tobacco, opium, rhubarb.   PLANTS VALUABLE FOR CLOTHING : Cotton, flax, hemp.

FIFTH YEAR OR GRADE

ZOÖLOGY, PHYSIOLOGY AND HYGIENE

First Quarter. Classification of animals, their differences and resemblances.   I. VERTEBRATES : *A.* Mammals : *a.* orang-outang, monkey ; *b.* bear, cat, dog, lion, panther, tiger, cougar, wolf, leopard ; *c.* kangaroo, opossum ; *d.* beaver, squirrel, rat, mouse ; *e.* sloth, ant-eater ; *f.* elephant, rhinoceros, hippopotamus, horse, hog ; *g.* camel, llama, camelopard, deer, goat, ox, sheep ; *h.* whale, dolphin, walrus, porpoise, seal.   *B.* Birds : *a.* vulture, eagle, hawk, owl ; *b.* parrot, woodpecker, cuckoo, toucan ; *c.* lark, robin, swallow, sparrow, mocking-bird ; *d.* domestic fowl, quail, pigeon, peacock, turkey, partridge ; *e.* ostrich, stork, crane, duck, swan, penguin, goose, pelican.

Second Quarter. Classification of animals continued. *C.* Reptiles : *a.* lizard, crocodile, allegator ; *b.* toad, frog, turtle ; *c.* rattlesnake, boa-constrictor, python, cobra. *D.* Fishes : pike, salmon, cod, mackerel, shad, shark, flying-fish, cat-fish, trout, herring, sardine. II. Molluscs : oyster, clam, pearl-oyster, snail. III. Articulates : lobster, craw-fish, worm, spider, insect (honey-bee, silk-worm, cochineal, fly, wasp, butterfly, etc.). IV. Radiates : corals, animalcules.

Second Quarter. Physiology and Hygiene : 1. Bones (preservation of the teeth) ; 2. Skin (its membranes, pores, perspiration, cleanliness) ; 3. flesh (fat, muscles, tendons) ; 4. Circulation of blood (veins, arteries, the heart) ; 5. Breathing (lungs, effect on the blood) ; 6. digestion (chyme, chyle, food and drink) ; 7. nerves (brain, five senses and how to use them) ; 8. Voluntary and involuntary motion, effect of exercise ; 9. Sleep, disease, death ; 10. Proper and improper hygienic habits (eating, drinking, sleeping, exercise, bathing, sitting in a draft of air, tight lacing, cramping the lungs, breathing pure air, keeping the feet warm and head cool, etc.)

Third Quarter. Physics : 1. Gravitation and pressure (weights, pump, barometer, pendulum) ;

2. Cohesion (glue, paste, mortar, cement, etc.); 3. Capillary attraction (lamp-wick, sap, sponge, sugar, etc.); 4. Mechanical powers (level, pulley, inclined plane, wedge and screw—friction). 5. Heat (sun, combustion, friction, effect on bodies, steam, thermometer, conduction, clothing, cooking, etc.); 6. Light (sources, reflection, looking-glass, refraction, spectacles, microscope, prism, telescope, effect on growing bodies, photograph); 7. Electricity (lightning, sealing-wax experiments, etc.); 8. Magnetism (mariner's compass, horse-shoe magnet, telegraph).

Fourth Quarter. ASTRONOMY : 1. Stars (some idea of size and distance(; 2. Solar system ; *a.* sun (source of light and heat, its size, spots); *b.* planets (their relative distances from the sun ; Venus and Jupiter, morning and evening star ; Saturn and his rings); *c.* satellites or moons (number of them); *d.* comets ; *e.* orbits (or paths of planets, moons, and comets) ; *f.* eclipses (of sun, of moon); *g.* seasons ; *h.* phases of moon.

SIXTH YEAR OR GRADE

OUTLINES OF PHYSICAL GEOGRAPHY

First Quarter. GEOLOGY : Structure of land, form of continents, islands, mountains and valleys, plateaus, plains, volcanoes, and earthquakes.

Second Quarter. THE WATER : Springs, rivers, lakes, the ocean, tides, waves, winds, currents, relation to commerce and climate.

Third Quarter. METEOROLOGY : The atmosphere, temperature, the winds, moisture of atmosphere, dew, fogs, rain, snow and hail, climate, electrical and optical phenomena of the atmosphere.

Fourth Quarter. ORGANIC LIFE : Botany, zoölogy, ethnography, relation of plants, animals and men to their place of abode.

SEVENTH YEAR OR GRADE

OUTLINES OF NATURAL PHILOSOPHY (OR PHYSICS), AS ILLUSTRATED IN FAMILIAR OBJECTS

First Quarter. Matter and its properties : force, molecular forces, gravitation and weight, specific gravity, centre of gravity, motion, action and reaction, compound motion.

Second Quarter. Machinery, friction, strength of materials, use of materials in construction, hydrostatics and capillary attraction, hydraulics, pneumatics, acoustics.

Third Quarter. Heat and its sources, communication and effects ; steam engine ; warming and ventilation ; meteorological instruments, thermometer; barometer, hydrometer, rain gauge, anemometer; classes of clouds; classes of winds; meteors and ærolites; aurora borealis; halos; circulation of water through the processes of evaporation, clouds, rain, springs, rivers, ocean, etc.

Fourth Quarter. Light: sources; reflection; prismatic spectrum; structure of the eye; optical instruments, telescope, microscope, etc; electricity, magnetism; electro-magnetism; telegraph.

ON THE METHOD OF TEACHING

1. The teacher must not consider herself required to go over all the topics assigned for any given quarter. She must not attempt to do any more than she can do in a proper manner. If it happens that only the first two or three topics are all that can be dealt with profitably, the teacher must not allow herself to undertake any more.

2. In case the teacher finds that the topics of any given quarter are not arranged in such an order that she can take them up to the best advantage, she is at liberty to change that order ; but she must not proceed to the work of a new quarter or to any portion of it until she has first given ten weekly lessons on the quarter's work she has begun.

3. No more than ten weekly lessons should be given on the work laid down for a quarter. When these have been given, proceed to the work of the next quarter, whether the topics of the quarter in hand have all been considered or only a very small portion of them.

REMARKS

The course is arranged with reference to *method* rather than quantity or exhaustiveness. If only one topic is thoroughly discussed in each quarter of the first year, some very important ideas will be gained of the science of botany. In the fourth year of the course, the pupil will come round to the subject again and can deepen his insight into the methods of studying the world of plants, learn the general outlines of classification adopted, and train his observing powers. When he comes to the sixth year of the course, he will again touch upon the subjects in such a manner as to see the province this subject occupies in the world of nature, and its general bearings upon other fields of investigation.

The question will be asked : Why not reduce the number of topics under a given subject to the number that can be actually discussed by the teacher?

The answer is : (1) A selection of topics from a comparatively full enumeration of them is best left to the individual teacher. (2) The exact number of topics that can be profitably discussed by teachers will vary with their capacities ; moreover, it will vary from year to year as teachers become familiar with the course; hence it is necessary to have a variety and to have topics enough for the most rapid classes. (3) It is, moreover, important to keep constantly before the teacher a full outline of the subject, so as to prevent the (very common) tendency to treat a theme in its narrow application only and to omit its general bearings.

GENERAL PLAN OF THE COURSE

It will be observed that in the seven years' course there is a spiral movement, or recurrence of the same topics : (1) The subjects of Natural Science, (a) the plant, (b) the animal, (c) the physical elements. and mechanical powers—constitute a primary course of three years ; so that even those who receive the minimum of school education shall acquire some insight into the elements and instrumentalities which play so important a part in the industrial age in which they live. (2) In the fourth and fifth years these subjects of Natural Science are all taken up again in a second course and much more scientifically developed : (a) Botany, its method and practical application ; (b) Zoölogy and Human Physiology ; (c) motion and force in masses, in particles, and as applied in the mechanical powers; (d) Astronomy (forming a transition to the grammar-school course in Physical Geography).   Five years is the average attendance in our schools; hence the average pupil will get two courses in Natural Science.   (3) In the sixth and seventh years of the district school a third course in Natural Science is given, in which begin to appear more clearly in outline the several sciences. (a) Under Natural History or organic nature: Geology, Meteorology, Botany, Zoölogy, Ethnology. (b) Under Natural Philosophy, or Physics: Matter, force and motion, machinery, molecular forces and instruments involving their application.

(4. In teaching Natural Science it is of the greatest importance to select typical objects or facts; *i. e.*, objects or phenomena that are types of a large class by reason of the fact that they manifest all of the chief properties or attributes common to the other individuals of the class, and at the same time manifest them in the most obvious manner.   It would not do, for instance, to select an object in which the properties to be illustrated were not well developed, nor an object with which the pupils were not familiar.)

5. Every lesson should be given in such a way as to draw out the perceptive powers of the pupil by leading him to reflect on what he sees, or to analyze

the object before him.   It is, at first thought, strange
—although it is true—that powers of observation are
to be strengthened only by teaching the pupil to
think upon what he sees.   The process is one of
division (analysis) and classification, and, secondly,
of tracing causal relations ; hence the questions most
frequent are : " What qualities or properties has this
object (exhibiting the same) ?   What separate actions
or movements form the steps or stages in a process ?
What other objects and processes have the same
(classification)?   What relation of this object or
phenomenon to others, whether as to cause and
effect or as to means and end ? "

6. *How to conduct a lesson :* (a) Prepare yourself
beforehand on the subject of the lesson of the week,
fixing in your mind exactly what subjects you will
bring up, just what definitions and illustrations you
will give or draw out of the class.   All must be
marked or written down in the form of a synopsis.
The blackboard is the most valuable appliance in
oral lessons ; on it should be written the technical
words discussed, the classification of the knowledge
brought out in the recitation, and, whenever possible,
illustrative drawings.   (b) Pains should be taken
to select passages from the reference book or from

other books illustrative of the subject under discussion, to be read to the class with explanation and conversation. (c) Whenever the subject is of such a nature as to allow of it, the teacher should bring in real objects illustrative of it and encourage the same. (d) But more stress should be laid on a direct appeal to their experience, encouraging them to describe what they have seen and heard, arousing habits of reflection, enabling the pupil to acquire a good command of language. (e) Great care must be taken by the teacher not to burden the pupil with too many technical phrases at a time, nor to fall into the opposite error of using only the loose common vocabulary of ordinary life, which lacks scientific precision.

7. *How to use the Reference Books.*

(a) *In the first course,* extending through the *seventh, sixth* and *fifth grades,* Hooker's Child's Book of Nature should be followed for the most part, with such hints as to method as are to be gained from a study of Calkins's Primary Object Lessons. SEVENTH GRADE. *First quarter :* Study and use such portions of the first ten chapters of Hooker's Part I. as you can make available. *Second quarter :* Chapters XI to XXI of the same book. *Third quarter :* Chapters

XXII to XXVII. *Fourth quarter:* Chapters XXIX to
XXXIII. SIXTH GRADE. *First quarter:* Chapters I
to VII of Hooker's Part II. *Second quarter:* Chapters VIII to XVIII. *Third quarter:* Chapters XIX to
XXV. *Fourth quarter:* Chapters XXVI to XXXIII.
FIFTH GRADE. *First quarter:* Chapters I to X of
Hooker's Part III. *Second quarter:* Chapters XI to
XVIII. *Third quarter:* Chapters XIX to XXXI. *Fourth
quarter:* Chapters XXXII to XXXV. Calkins's Object
Lessons, pp. 15 to 50, should be studied in the
seventh grade; pp. 401 to 431 will be of great service
in the *sixth grade;* and the same book, pp. 139 to
190 and pp. 339 to 400, will be of equal service in
the *fifth grade.*

(b) In the second course, extending through the
fourth and *third grades,* Youmans's First Book in
Botany should be studied for method and material
for the lessons given in the *first quarter* of the
FOURTH GRADE. Only a few selections can be
made on account of lack of time, but these should
be of the most suggestive order. For *second, third*
and *fourth quarters* of the FOURTH GRADE, Warren's
Physical Geography will furnish classification, description and facts (pp. 70 to 78, new edition).
THIRD GRADE. *First quarter:* Warren's Physical

Geography, pp. 78 to 85. *Second quarter:* Refer to Draper's Physiology for information; use "Syllabus of Physiology" for further suggestions. *Third quarter:* Use Hotze's First Lessons in Physics for method, and Wells's Natural Philosophy for information. *Fourth quarter:* Use Warren's Physical Geography, pp. 5 to 8, and Steele's Fourteen Weeks in Astronomy.

(c) In the third course, extending through the *second* and *first grades*, Warren's Physical Geography should be used for the first year, and Wells's Natural Philosophy for the second year. Constant reference should be made to Tate's Natural Philosophy, Brande's Dictionary, and other books. The Public School Library is free to teachers as a Reference Library. A set of colored illustration-charts is given to each school; many things can be best taught by means of charts.

8. Although instruction in Natural Science is limited to one hour per week, yet it is expected that what is taught in these lessons will be referred to frequently in the regular Course of Study. Whenever, for instance, any of the subjects treated in this course of instruction come up in teaching the other branches, an exposition of their scientific

phases should be required of the pupils. This will apply to the subject of Geography more than to the others. Arithmetic, History, and the Reading lesson will occasionally furnish references to one or more provinces here mapped out.

9. In connection with the Geography, History, and Grammar lessons a study of MAN should be carried on parallel to the study of material nature of the weekly oral lessons. The outlines of study embrace: *1st.* Physiology, or science of man as a body; this comes under Natural Science; *2d,* Ethnology, or study of man as conditioned in development by his surroundings, climate, race, etc.; *3d,* Wants and necessities of food, clothing, shelter, and the relation of these to the world, animal, vegetable, and mineral; *4th,* Language and its divisions and structure; *5th,* States of Society; *6th,* Employments and occupations; *7th,* Government; *8th,* Religions.

10. Compositions should be written subsequent to the oral lessons, on the topics discussed. They should be short and to the point, and always in the pupil's own words.

11. *Resumé.* To name once more in a brief

manner the cardinal points to be kept in mind constantly by the teacher :

(a) Take up only so many of the topics laid down for any given quarter as can be discussed thoroughly without overburdening the pupil's memory or distracting his power of attention.

(b) Never take up a topic that you are unable to explain and illustrate so clearly as to make the pupil understand it ; avoid all phases of the subject that will tend to confuse rather than enlighten.

(c) Spend only ten weeks on the work of a given quarter, whether you do little or much in it ; proceed then to the topics of the next quarter.

(d) Relieve the hour's work by as much variety as possible : *first*, reading and explaining something adapted to the capacity of your pupils ; *secondly*, drawing out in conversational manner the experience and information which your scholars already possess on the subject ; *thirdly*, exhibiting the visible objects which you or the pupils have brought to illustrate the lesson, and requiring the pupils to notice and name the properties, qualities, parts, and attributes ; *fourthly*, never omitting to show by a synopsis on the blackboard what has been discussed in the lesson, its classification and relation.

(e) Require short weekly compositions of the pupils above the fifth grade, in which they express in their own language their ideas on the subjects treated in the oral lessons.

www.ingramcontent.com/pod-product-compliance
Lightning Source LLC
Chambersburg PA
CBHW032135080426
42733CB00008B/1085